CyberSmarts
STAYING SAFE ONLINE

Avoiding Predators Online

Bonnie Spivet

PowerKiDS press™

New York

Published in 2012 by The Rosen Publishing Group
29 East 21st Street, New York, NY 10010

First Edition

Editor: Karolena Bielecki
Book Design: Erica Clendening

Photo credits: Cover © www.istockphoto.com/Grady Reese; p. 4 © www.
istockphoto.com/Hope Milam; p. 7 Thomas Barwick/Taxi/Getty Images;
pp. 8, 13 Shutterstock.com; p. 11 © www.istockphoto.com/Margot Petrowski;
p. 15 © www.istockphoto.com/Cat London; p. 17 SW Productions/Photodisc/
Getty Images; p. 18 Joe Raedle/Getty Images; p. 21 Simon Winnall/Taxi/
Getty Images.

Library of Congress Cataloging-in-Publication Data

Spivet, Bonnie.
Avoiding predators online / by Bonnie Spivet.—1st ed.
     p. cm—(Cybersmarts: staying safe online)
Includes index.
ISBN 978-1-4488-6411-9 (library binding)—ISBN 978-1-4488-6416-4 (pbk.)—
ISBN 978-1-4488-6417-1 (6-pack)
1. Internet and children—Juvenile literature. 2. Internet—Safety measures
—Juvenile literature. 3. Computer crimes—Prevention—Juvenile literature.
I. Title.
HQ784.I58S66 2012
004.67'8083—dc23

                                                           2011017344

Manufactured in the United States of America

CPSIA Compliance Information: Batch #W12PK: For further information, contact Rosen Publishing, New York, New York, at
1–800–237–9932.

Contents

Be Aware

You are lucky to live in the age of the Internet. It is a great tool for learning about any topic. You can use it to keep in touch with family and friends. You can play games online, too. With so many things to discover, though, you need to remember to be safe.

Being online should be fun, but a message from an online predator can be upsetting. Messages from these people can contain pictures and text that a kid should not read.

When you are in public, you watch out for strangers. When you are online, you need to do this, too. There are bad people who may use the Internet to try to meet children. They are called predators. They try to become friends with kids and ask them to do things that kids should not do. If you know how to avoid online predators, you can stay safe and have fun online.

Predator Warning Signs

Not everyone is a safe online buddy. Always be careful when talking to people online. They may be pretending to be other people if they:

- Agree with everything you say. A predator will try to make you feel good about yourself.
- Ask you your age, address, or other **private** questions.
- Ask for your phone number or ask you to call or send them a **text message**.
- Ask to meet in person.
- Tell you to keep the friendship a secret.
- Offer you gifts.

If someone does these things, ignore or block him and tell an adult right away.

Strangers Online

Predators use **chat rooms** and other places where kids hang out online. After predators join chats, they send private messages to kids. They leave notes on Web sites and send messages by e-mail. Predators sometimes talk to kids while they are playing games online, too.

If a predator **contacts** you, the first messages may sound like they are from a buddy. The messages will seem friendly at first. Then, the predator may ask for your real name or age.

Never answer questions from a stranger. Do not even write back. It is okay to ignore any message that makes you uncomfortable. It is not rude. It is being safe. You should not open or answer messages from people you do not know.

Do not read any message you think might be from an online predator. If you feel unsafe or uncomfortable, move on to a different Web site or chat room or ignore the e-mail.

Steer Clear

Knowing about online predators is the first step to staying safe. You can also do things to avoid them. Telling anyone online your real name, age, or where you live is a bad idea. Never put this **information** in **online profiles**. Keep facts such as your school name, team names, phone

The Internet is a great place to learn and hang out, but do not share too much about yourself. Always think before you post or click "send."

number, and e-mail address to yourself, too. These can all be used to find you.

Visit only those chat rooms that have a **moderator**, or an adult who reads the chats. Do not post pictures of yourself online unless you ask an adult first. Share your e-mail address and **screen names** only with your family and good friends.

Know Your Network

There are a lot of places to meet with your friends online. A **social network**, such as Facebook, is a place where people go to share their interests, chat, and post pictures. Social networks are sites where you can talk with friends. Not all social networks are okay for all ages. For example, Facebook users must be at least 13 years old.

Some kids break these rules and sign up anyway. Do not do this. It is dangerous to join a site for older people. You could become the target of a predator. Social networks do not let kids join for a good reason. They want to keep you safe.

You Never Know

When you see people in person, you can tell a lot about them. You can see how old they are. You can hear their voices. You know if they are boys or girls. This is not true online. People can make up **identities**. They can pick new names. They can lie about their ages. People can lie about where they live, too. They can even use other people's pictures as their own pictures.

No matter how many times you chat with a person online, remember that you do not know who that person really is. You may feel like you know the person, but you do not. Online predators often pretend to be people they are not. They may even pretend to be kids.

Do not believe everything you read. Remember that you cannot tell if people are being honest online.

Tricks and Traps

A predator will try to earn your trust and become your friend. Predators might agree with things you tell them and pretend to have the same interests as you. Predators may send messages in which they try to get more information from you. The more you talk to predators, the more they will contact you.

Predators often ask if they can send pictures to you. They may also want you to send pictures of yourself to them. Never accept or send pictures. Instead, tell an adult. Predators may even ask you to do things that make you feel uncomfortable. It can be upsetting to get messages from a predator. You did nothing wrong, though. Do not be afraid to tell an adult you trust.

You do not need to be afraid to go online. Stay smart and use your head. Remember the warning signs that someone dangerous might be contacting you.

Put a Stop to It

If an online predator targets you, remember that it is not your fault. It does not matter if the message comes in a chat room, by e-mail, or while you are playing a game. Do not feel **embarrassed** or trapped. Instead, put a stop to the messages.

If someone online makes you uncomfortable, end contact with that person at once. Do not let the predator know that you are going to tell anyone what happened. Instead, tell a trusted adult. Predators may try to **manipulate** you or make you feel bad. They may try to change your mind. Go online with the adult and show him the messages that you received. Tell the adult everything that happened. Together, make a plan to keep you away from the predator.

A predator may try to make you feel bad or guilty about the messages they send you. Do not be afraid to show a parent or other adult you trust. She can help protect you from harm.

The Law

Online predators are criminals. It is against the law to send **inappropriate** pictures or movies to a kid. In Canada, there is a law against luring or **exploiting** children under the age of 14. It is also a crime to contact people again and again and make them feel unsafe. This is called **harassment**.

If anyone asks you to do something that feels wrong, tell an adult who can contact the police. It is normal to feel uncomfortable and scared. You have done nothing wrong and are not in trouble. Police know how to deal with predators.

Tell the police about everything that a predator sent you. Do not share these things with friends. Instead, ask the police what you should do with them.

Talking to the police about an online predator might seem scary. Talk to an adult you trust first. It will make talking to an officer easier. Remember, the police are there to help.

What the Police Can Do

Do not be afraid to tell a police officer everything about an online predator. The police may also ask to check your computer. This will let them look at messages that you have received from a predator. They may find clues to the predator's identity.

Police officers can find important evidence on the computer of an online predator. Computers are usually seized, or taken away, when a predator is arrested.

Police officers have many ways to catch an online predator. They use the messages that kids report. Sometimes officers pretend to be kids in chat rooms and talk to online predators. This is called a sting operation. The police officer may try to set up real-life meetings with predators. When the predators show up, the police officers **arrest** them. When you tell police about an online predator, you are helping keep other kids safe, too.

Government Protection

The government has laws to protect kids online. In the United States, the Children's Internet Protection Act (CIPA) was passed in 2000. It requires some schools and public libraries to have Internet filters. The Internet filters block content not safe for people under age 18.

The Deleting Online Predators Act (DOPA) is a bill that would stop access to "commercial social networking sites" and chat rooms. Some people believe it would block access to useful, educational sites, too, though.

In Canada, the National Child Exploitation Coordination Centre works hard to fight and stop online exploitation of children. In 2002, Canada passed a law against luring or exploiting children under the age of 14. Some forms of online harassment are criminal acts under Canadian law. It is against the law to communicate repeatedly with people if what you say makes them afraid for their safety.

Be Web Wise

You do not need to be afraid of being online. You do need to be smart about it, though. Before you log on, talk with your parents or guardian. Together, agree on a list of rules and sites that are safe to visit. One very important rule every kid should have is that you will never meet a person whom you met online in person.

You already know how to be safe at the mall or the park. The Internet is the same in many ways. You must be careful of strangers. You should not go to unfamiliar places. You should stay in places that are safe for kids. Be safe while you surf, and you can have a lot of fun online.

Spend some time visiting sites with a parent. Together you can find Web sites that are safe and fun and free of online predators.

Safety Tips

- Never agree to meet someone in person whom you met online.

- Pick a screen name that hides your real identity.

- Do not share your **passwords** with your friends or with people you meet online.

- Never give out your phone number or call a number that was given to you by someone you met online.

- Open messages only from people you know.

- If something in a message does not seem right, tell an adult.

- Remember that you can never really know to whom you are talking when you are online.

- Never post a photo online without asking an adult first.

- Talk to a trusted adult before visiting sites that let you talk to strangers.

arrest (uh-REST) To catch people who are thought to have committed crimes.

chat rooms (CHAT ROOMZ) Online places where people can type messages to each other.

contacts (KON-takts) Talks or meets with a person.

embarrassed (em-BAR-usd) Full of shame or uneasiness.

exploiting (ik-SPLOYT-ing) Using in a harmful or unfair way.

harassment (huh-RAS-ment) Repeated aggression or pressure.

identities (eye-DEN-tuh-teez) Traits that make people who they are.

inappropriate (in-nuh-PROH-pree-ut) Not suitable or right.

information (in-fer-MAY-shun) Knowledge or facts.

manipulate (muh-NIH-pyuh-layt) To influence or control a person.

moderator (MO-deh-ray-tur) Someone who monitors a chat room or Web site forum.

online profiles (AWN-lyn PROH-fy-elz) Information about themselves that people enter to be stored on Web sites.

passwords (PAS-wurdz) Secret combinations of letters or numbers that let people enter something.

private (PRY-vit) Meant to be seen or known only by certain people.

screen names (SKREEN NAYMZ) Names people use online.

social network (SO-shul net-WERK) A Web site where people connect with friends and family online.

text message (TEKST MEH-sij) A written message sent by cellular phone.

Index

A

address, 5, 9
adult, 5, 9, 12, 14, 16, 22
age(s), 4–6, 8–10, 16, 19

B

buddy, 5–6

C

Canada, 16, 19
chat room(s), 6, 9,
  14, 19
chats, 6, 9
children, 5, 16, 19

F

family, 4, 9
friend(s), 4–5, 9, 12,
  16, 22

G

game(s), 4, 6, 14

H

harassment, 16, 19

I

identities, 10, 18, 22
information, 8, 12
Internet, 4–5, 19, 20

K

kid(s), 5–6, 9–10, 16,
  19–20

M

message(s), 5–6, 12,
  14, 18–19, 22

P

phone number, 5,
  8–9, 22

pictures, 9–10,
  12, 16
police officer(s), 16,
  18–19

Q

questions, 5–6

S

screen name(s), 9, 22
social network(s), 9
stranger(s), 5–6,
  20, 22

T

text message, 5
topic, 4

W

Web site(s), 6, 9,
  19–20, 22

Web Sites

Due to the changing nature of Internet links, PowerKids Press has developed an online list of Web sites related to the subject of this book. This site is updated regularly. Please use this link to access the list:

www.powerkidslinks.com/cyber/predator